THE SPIRIT OF CHRISTMAS

To my parents, Gordon and Janel Olsen,
whose holiday traditions filled our home with
all the uplifting magic and wonder that, for
me, nurtured the true Spirit of Christmas.

Text and artwork © 2024 Greg Olsen

Visit us at shadowmountain.com

Library of Congress Cataloging-in-Publication Data
CIP data on file
ISBN 978-1-63993-344-0

Printed in the United States of America
Phoenix Color, Hagerstown, MD 5/2024

10   9   8   7   6   5   4   3   2

THE SPIRIT OF

CHRISTMAS

GREG OLSEN

SHADOW
MOUNTAIN
PUBLISHING

By the magical light of a small Christmas candle

a little old man tries to carefully handle

The small porcelain manger which serves as a bed
for the wee Baby Jesus to lay down His head.

In wonder, he brings the manger up to his view,

smiles at the baby and whispers, "I love you!"

I love you for bringing this season of joy;

I love you for growing to a man from a boy;

For being our light and leading the way,

for being the spirit which makes Christmas Day!

*Y*ou've been my mentor, my model, my hero and guide.

Please continue to help me and stay by my side.

I've tried to follow your teachings and give as you gave,

reminding all to be kind, and that it's wise to behave.

*H*elp me to serve others and bring them your light,
especially the children—please bless them tonight!

Some have so very little, scarce food for their table.

You know how it feels—you were born in a stable!

*B*less all their mothers and fathers with knowledge that's sure;

the best gift they can give is their love, strong and pure.

That's the Spirit of Christmas when all's said and done,

God's gift of love, that came as His Son!

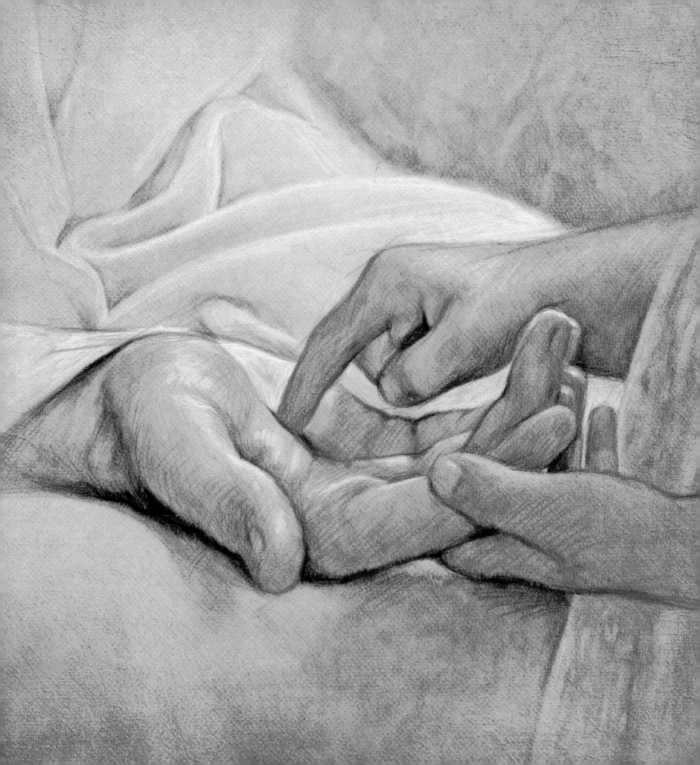

Then back to His mother the Child is returned.

The Nativity glows as the candle is burned.

In a wink, the little old man slips quietly away.

Some say he goes up the chimney and climbs in his sleigh.

Whatever the case, his mission is clear—

give unto others, bringing love and good cheer.

$\mathcal{H}$e flies into the night and bids us adieu . . .

doing for others what Jesus would do!